Hell's Kitchen Cookbook

Can You Impress Gordon?

BY

M. Gilb

License Notes

No part of this Book can be reproduced in any form or by any means including print, electronic, scanning or photocopying unless prior permission is granted by the author.

All ideas, suggestions and guidelines mentioned here are written for informative purposes. While the author has taken every possible step to ensure accuracy, all readers are advised to follow information at their own risk. The author cannot be held responsible for personal and/or commercial damages in case of misinterpreting and misunderstanding any part of this Book

Table of Contents

Introduction 6

Chapter 1: Drinks to Get the Party Started! 8

   1.Bourbon... 9

   2.Oak Scotch.. 11

   3.Ginger Beer 13

   4.Sweet Vermouth 15

   5.Gin 17

   6.Peach Lemonade 19

Chapter 2: Starters and Main Course 21

   7.Beef Wellington... 22

   8.Seared Scallops 25

   9.Crispy Salmon 27

   10.Lamb Chops... 29

   11.Risotto 31

12.Lobster Spaghetti 34

13.Truffle Carbonara 36

14.Grilled Bone-In Pork 38

15.Pan Roasted Halibut 40

16.Crispy Skin Duck Breast 42

17.Herb Crusted Lamb 44

18.Baked Chicken Breast 46

19.Lemon Tagliatelle 48

20.Herb Oil infused Fish 50

21.Old Fashioned Chicken Soup 52

22.Seared Branzino 54

23.Brick Chicken 56

24.South Western Style Beef Fillet 58

25.Avocado Mousse 61

26.Roasted Apple Tart 63

27.Tiramisu 65

28.Bread Pudding 67

29.Goji Berry and Apple Compote 69

30.Raspberry Salad 71

Conclusion 73

Introduction

Do you love Hell's Kitchen? Are you a fan of Gordon Ramsey? Do you want a menu inspiration for your dinner party? This book is your best resource!

The contestants on the show might split hair coming up with a menu to impress Gordon, but you don't have to. The book will leave you with delicious recipes that will impress your family and guests.

From lip-smacking cocktails to delicious main courses and delectable desserts, there are a lot to choose from. You will wonder if you should serve chicken or beef or settle for a fish dish!

The recipes are perfect for Thanksgiving and even Christmas!

So, without wasting any more time, let's go straight in!

Chapter 1: Drinks to Get the Party Started!

1.Bourbon

The drink menu at Hell's Kitchen is quite diverse. Here is one with Bourbon.

Serving size: 1

Cooking time: 5 minutes

Ingredients:

- 2 ounces Bourbon
- 1 ounce maple syrup
- 1 ounce lemon juice
- Cherry to garnish
- Ice cubes

Instructions:

Add bourbon, syrup and lemon juice to a shaker along with ice cubes and shake for 15 seconds.

Serve with a cherry.

2.Oak Scotch

Oak Scotch has a strong woody flavor. Here is a rustic cocktail to try out.

Serving size: 1

Cooking time: 5 minutes

Ingredients:

- ¼ ounce cinnamon sugar syrup
- 2 ounces Oak Scotch
- 2 dashes Angostura bitters
- Orange peel
- Ice cubes

Instructions:

Add cinnamon syrup, Scotch, bitters and ice cubes to a shaker and shake for 15 seconds.

Pour into a glass. Garnish with an orange peel and serve.

3.Ginger Beer

Ginger beer has a unique taste and very little alcohol content. It can be used to make delicious cocktails.

Serving size: 1

Cooking time: 5 minutes

Ingredients:

- ½ ounce lime juice
- 2 ounces tequila
- 4 ounces ginger beer
- Ice cubes
- Lime to garnish

Instructions:

Add lime juice, tequila, ginger beer and ice to a shaker and shake for 15 seconds.

Pour into a glass. Garnish with a lime wedge and serve.

4.Sweet Vermouth

Sweet vermouth has a sweet aniseed flavor, making it perfect for sweet cocktails.

Serving size: 1

Cooking time: 5 minutes

Ingredients:

- 2 ounces Bourbon
- 1 ounce sweet vermouth
- 2 dashes bitters
- 1 dash orange bitter
- Ice cubes
- Cherry to garnish

Instructions:

Add bourbon, vermouth, bitters, orange bitter and ice to a shaker and shake for 15 seconds.

Serve with a cherry in the glass.

5.Gin

Made using Juniper berries, gin is an alcoholic drink that monks used for its medicinal properties. Gin is often served with lemon.

Serving size: 1

Cooking time: 5 minutes

Ingredients:

- 1 ounce lime syrup
- Ice cubes
- 2 ounces dry gin
- Lime to garnish

Instructions:

Add syrup, gin and ice cubes to a shaker and shake for 5 seconds.

Pour in a glass and garnish with lime and serve.

6.Peach Lemonade

Peach lemonade is a delicious refresher. It is perfect for all seasons and a great drink to serve at your party.

Serving size: 4-5

Cooking time: 10 minutes

Ingredients:

- 4 cups water
- 1 cup honey/sugar
- 1 cup lemon juice
- 1 lemon, sliced
- Mint leaves
- 2 peaches, chopped

Instructions:

Boil 2 cups water and add peaches and sugar.

Simmer for 5 minutes until peaches are soft.

Peel the peaches and add to a blender with lemon juice, water and the boiled water and whizz till smooth.

Add to a pitcher with lemon slices, mint leaves and ice cubes and stir.

Serve cold.

Chapter 2: Starters and Main Course

7.Beef Wellington

Every season of Hell's Kitchen has to have a beef Wellington recipe. It's a classic dish of cooked beef wrapped inside puff pastry. Gordon is hardly ever impressed and tosses an entire batch into the bin. But don't worry, this recipe will help you make a delicious beef wellington dish!

Serving size: 4

Cooking time: 1 hour

Ingredients:

- 2 lb beef tenderloin
- 2 tablespoons oil
- 2 tablespoons mustard
- 2 lb mushrooms, chopped
- 1 shallot, chopped
- 1 tablespoon thyme leaves
- 2 tablespoons butter
- 12 prosciutto slices
- 14 ounces puff pastry
- 1 egg, beaten
- Flour for dusting
- Salt and pepper to taste

Instructions:

Add tenderloin to a plate and sprinkle salt and pepper.

Add oil toa skillet and brown the tenderloin.

Finely chop shallots, mushrooms and thyme.

Add butter to a skillet and add the above three ingredients and cook till brown.

Place the prosciutto slices on a plate and apply the mushroom mixture on top.

Place the tenderloin over it and wrap it with the prosciutto.

Roll the puff pastry out such that it can cover the entire tenderloin.

Tightly wrap the tenderloin and brush it with an egg wash.

Place in a preheated 425 Fahrenheit oven and bake for 50 minutes.

Slice and serve.

8.Seared Scallops

Gordon loves seared scallops. He often insists that the perfect way to get them right seared is to maintain the ideal temperature of the pan.

Serving size: 4-6

Cooking time: 10 minutes

Ingredients:

- ½ lb sea scallops
- 1 tablespoon avocado oil
- 2 tablespoons butter
- Salt and pepper to taste

Instructions:

Add scallops to a plate and season with salt and pepper.

Heat a skillet and add a tablespoon oil.

Cook the scallops for no more than 2-3 minutes on both sides.

Dip a brush in the butter and coat the scallops.

Serve warm.

9.Crispy Salmon

One of the popular dishes on the show is crispy salmon. Gordon enjoys the crunch of the crispy skin of salmon.

Serving size: 4

Cooking time: 30 minutes

Ingredients:

- 30 ounces salmon filets
- 2 tablespoons lemon juice
- 1 tablespoon oil
- 2 tablespoons butter
- 1 tablespoon garlic, minced
- 4 tablespoons parsley leaves, chopped
- Salt and pepper to taste

Instructions:

Add the salmon to a plate and pat it dry.

Sprinkle salt and pepper and pour lemon juice all over.

Heat oil in a pan and press the fish down over it and fry till crispy golden.

Gradually flip it over and fry the other side.

Add butter and garlic around the fillet and sizzle.

Add parsley leaves and serve warm.

10.Lamb Chops

Lamb chops look simply but are not an easy dish to pull off. It is a part of every Hell's kitchen season, and Gordon loves to criticize the contestants.

Serving size: 8

Cooking time: 1 hour

Ingredients:

- 1 lemon, juiced
- 2 teaspoons oregano
- 1 tablespoon garlic, minced
- ¼ cup oil
- 8 lamb chops
- Salt and pepper to taste

Instructions:

Add lemon juice, oregano, 1 tablespoon oil, salt and pepper and lamb to a bowl and marinate it for 30 minutes.

Heat oil in a pot. Then, fry the lamb chops in batches until crispy brown.

Drain on tissues and serve.

11.Risotto

Indeed, risotto is an Italian rice dish that is slightly difficult to pull off. It requires patience and some elbow grease. Gordon is often dissatisfied with what the contestants put out.

Serving size: 4

Cooking time: 40 minutes

Ingredients:

- 4 tablespoons butter
- 1 onion, chopped
- 4 cups warm chicken broth
- 1 tablespoon garlic, minced
- 2 cups arborio rice
- 3 cups water
- ¼ cup white wine
- 1 cup parmesan cheese, grated
- Salt and pepper to taste
- 2 tablespoons chives
- 2 tablespoons basil leaves

Instructions:

Add water to a pot and boil.

Melt butter in a pan. Then, cook onions and garlic till soft.

Add rice and salt and toast the rice.

Pour wine and boil.

Reduce the flame and add a ladleful of warm broth and stir until the broth is absorbed.

Add another ladleful and wait for it to absorb.

Continue doing this until all the broth is absorbed.

Remove from flame and add butter and pepper and mix.

Sprinkle chives, basil and parmesan and serve.

12.Lobster Spaghetti

Lobster spaghetti is a classic spaghetti dish. It is delicious to taste and perfect for a classy party.

Serving size: 2

Cooking time: 30 minutes

Ingredients:

- 1 lb lobster, cooked
- 3 tablespoons oil
- 1 tablespoon garlic, minced
- ½ cup tomatoes, chopped
- 1 lb spaghetti, cooked al dente
- Parsley leaves, chopped
- Chili, chopped
- Salt and pepper to taste

Instructions:

Place the lobster on a flat surface and use a sharp knife to cut it lengthwise into two.

Cut the tails and remove the flesh.

Add oil to a pan. Toss in garlic and brown.

Add tomatoes, salt, chili and pepper and spaghetti and toss.

Add the lobster meat. Then, cook for 2 minutes.

Serve with a sprinkling of parsley.

13.Truffle Carbonara

One of the first few dishes made on the show, truffle carbonara is a delicious dish made using truffle butter and freshly shaved truffles.

Serving size: 4

Cooking time: 30 minutes

Ingredients:

- 1 teaspoon garlic, minced
- 1 tablespoon butter
- ¼ cup wine
- 1/3 cup cream
- 1 egg
- 1 egg yolk
- ½ cup parmesan cheese
- 2 tablespoons parsley
- 1 lb pasta
- Salt and pepper to taste
- Fresh black and white truffles

Instructions:

Cook the pasta till al dente.

Add butter and garlic to a pan and sauté till brown.

Pour the wine and cook till it evaporates.

Add cream and pasta and mix.

Add the eggs, yolk, salt and pepper to a bowl and whisk till well combined.

Pour it over the pasta and stir till the egg scrambles.

Serve with a sprinkling of parsley.

14.Grilled Bone-In Pork

Season 1 of the show certainly introduced us to a whole host of recipes. One of them is the grilled bone-in pork that is juicy and succulent and perfect for

Serving size: 4

Cooking time: 30 minutes

Ingredients:

- ¼ cup honey
- 1 cup water
- 1 tablespoon apple cider vinegar
- Salt and pepper to taste
- 6 ounces pork chops, bone-in
- 1 tablespoon oil

Instructions:

Add honey, water, vinegar, pepper and salt to a bowl and mix till well combined.

Add the pork chops and marinate it for an hour.

Preheat a grill to 500 and grill the chops on both sides.

Baste it with the oil using a brush or spoon.

Grill for about 4 minutes on both sides.

Allow it to rest for 5 minutes. S

15.Pan Roasted Halibut

Nothing like moist halibut with crispy skin over it. It pairs well with red wine and makes for an exquisite dish. Remember, the more expensive the fish, the moister it stays.

Serving size: 4

Cooking time: 30 minutes

Ingredients:

- 2 lb halibut fillets, cut into 2 inches thick pieces
- Salt and pepper to taste
- 3 tablespoons olive oil

Instructions:

Place the fish on a plate and dry it using tissues if it's moist.

Season it with salt and pepper and rub both sides.

Heat a pan. Add oil and sear the skin side of the fish and flip it around after 5 minutes.

Transfer it to a baking tray and bake in a preheated 150 Fahrenheit oven for 10 minutes.

16.Crispy Skin Duck Breast

If you are bored of serving turkey every year for thanksgiving, then here is something different for you to try out. Consider serving this duck dish and surprise your family and guests.

Serving size: 2

Cooking time: 30 minutes

Ingredients:

- 1 tablespoon oil
- 2 lb duck breasts, 4 breasts
- Salt and pepper to taste

Instructions:

First, place the duck breast on a plate. Using a sharp knife, carefully score the skin in a criss-cross pattern.

Sprinkle salt and pepper over it and rub it in.

Heat the oil over a skillet and place the duck breasts on top.

Next, place the duck skin-side down and sear it till golden.

Cook for 8 to 10 minutes approximately until soft and crispy golden.

Once the fat starts to release, transfer it to a baking tray and bake in a preheated 450 Fahrenheit oven for 10 minutes.

Slice and serve.

17.Herb Crusted Lamb

Herb crusted rack of lamb is an exquisite dish. It is visually appealing and great to taste. It is a common dish served in Hell's Kitchen.

Serving size: 4

Cooking time: 30 minutes

Ingredients:

- 3 lb rack lamb
- Salt and pepper to taste
- 4 tablespoons oil
- 2 tablespoons garlic, minced
- 1 cup breadcrumbs
- ¼ cup parsley
- ½ cup parmesan, grated
- 2 tablespoons rosemary
- 2 tablespoons mustard

Instructions:

Add the lamb to a plate and season it with salt and pepper.

Heat a cast-iron pan and add 3 tablespoons of oil.

Sear all sides of the lamb till crispy and add it to a baking tray.

Next, add garlic, parsley, breadcrumbs, rosemary, 1 tablespoon oil and parmesan to a bowl and mix.

Apply mustard over the lamb and coat it with the breadcrumbs mixture.

Roast it in a preheated 450 Fahrenheit oven for 30 minutes.

Lastly, allow it to cool before slicing and serving.

18.Baked Chicken Breast

Nothing like this easy to make a dish that is high on flavor. All you need is some herbs, spices and chicken breast, and you can put them together to make the delicious dish. Here is its simple recipe to follow.

Serving size: 4

Cooking time: 30 minutes

Ingredients:

- 4 boneless, skinless chicken breasts
- 1 tablespoon butter
- Salt and pepper to taste
- 1 teaspoon garlic, minced
- 1 large egg
- ½ teaspoon paprika

Instructions:

First, add the chicken to a bowl along with warm water and salt.

Allow it to sit for 15 minutes.

Next, remove and pat the chicken dry and place it on a baking tray.

Add butter to a pan and place the chicken over it.

Mix egg, salt, pepper, garlic and paprika and apply it generously over the chicken.

Next, bake in a preheated 350 Fahrenheit oven for 20 minutes.

Allow it to rest for 10 minutes.

Serve warm.

19.Lemon Tagliatelle

Undoubtedly, this is a quick and easy dish that is big on taste. It is one of the most common and popular dishes on the show.

Serving size: 4

Cooking time: 30 minutes

Ingredients:

- 2 lemons, juiced and zested
- 4 tablespoons oil
- 1 lb tagliatelle
- ½ cup cheese, grated
- Rocket leaves, roughly torn
- Salt and pepper to taste

Instructions:

Cook the tagliatelle until al dente.

Add lemon juice, zest, salt, pepper and oil to a bowl and mix.

Toss in the tagliatelle along with cheese and mix.

Serve with rocket leaves on top.

20.Herb Oil infused Fish

One of the best ways to flavor by using herb-infused oil. Here is a recipe that impressed Gordon.

Serving size: 4

Cooking time: 30 minutes

Ingredients:

- 1 tablespoon garlic, minced
- 1 cup parsley
- 1 cup mint leaves
- ¼ cup oregano leaves
- 1/3 cup oil
- 4 fish fillets
- 1 large lemon
- Bread to serve

Instructions:

Zest and juice the lemon. Then, add to a bowl.

Add the oregano, mint and parsley leaves, garlic and oil and mix.

Add it to a pan and add the fish.

Fry both sides until the fish is cooked and infused with the oil.

Serve with bread.

21.Old Fashioned Chicken Soup

Gordon is hard to please, but he loves it when someone serves traditional meals. He particularly enjoys soups.

Serving size: 4

Cooking time: 30 minutes

Ingredients:

- 5 lb chicken, chopped
- 2 onions, chopped
- 4 celery sticks, chopped
- 1 tablespoon garlic, minced
- 4 carrots, chopped
- 2 bay leaves
- 1 teaspoon thyme
- 2 teaspoons parsley
- 4 cups stock/water
- Salt and pepper to taste
- Chives to sprinkle

Instructions:

Add chicken and stock to a pot and cook till soft.

Once cooked, remove the chicken to a plate.

Add the garlic, herbs, salt and pepper to the pot and boil.

Add the chicken back to the pot and simmer for 5 minutes.

Remove the bay leaves and serve with the soup with chives sprinkled on top.

22.Seared Branzino

As you might certainly have noticed, one of the most popular ingredients to cook with on the show is fish. Branzino is a variety of European fish that is popular on the show.

Serving size: 4

Cooking time: 30 minutes

Ingredients:

- 4 Branzino fillets, de-boned
- Salt and pepper to taste
- 2 tablespoons oil
- 1 cup cherry tomatoes, halved
- ½ cup olives, halved
- 3 tablespoons white wine
- 1 tablespoon butter
- 2 tablespoons parsley

Instructions:

Using a sharp knife, score lines over the fillet and sprinkle salt and pepper over it.

Heat oil on a skillet and roast the fish skin side down.

Add the tomatoes and olives to a saucepan and cook for a minute.

Pour the wine, butter and parsley and simmer.

Drizzle it over the fish and serve.

23.Brick Chicken

Brick chicken is a classic dish that was showcased in the recipes from Hell's Kitchen season 2. It has a unique taste and perfect for parties.

Serving size: 4

Cooking time: 30 minutes

Ingredients:

- 2 whole chicken, halved
- 1 tablespoon olive oil
- Salt and pepper to taste
- 1 tablespoon butter
- 5 thyme sprigs

Instructions:

Clean and refrigerate the chicken and pat it dry.

Season it with salt and pepper.

Add oil, thyme and butter to a skillet and roast the chicken till golden.

Cover the chicken with a bowl or vessel such that it seals the chicken.

Lower the heat and cook for 10 minutes.

Flip it around and cook with the cover for 5 minutes.

Slice and serve.

24.South Western Style Beef Fillet

One of the signature dishes on the show that impressed Gordon is the South Western Style Beef Fillet.

Serving size: 4

Cooking time: 30 minutes

Ingredients:

- 3 lb beef tenderloin, trimmed
- 2 tablespoons oil
- Salt and pepper to taste
- 1 tablespoon garlic, minced
- 3 tablespoons shallots, chopped
- 2 tablespoons tomato paste
- 3 tablespoons mustard
- 2 cups chicken broth
- 3 tablespoons maple syrup
- ¼ cup vinegar
- 3 teaspoons cilantro
- 2 tablespoons jalapenos to sprinkle

Instructions:

Cut the beef into ½ inch medallions and season it with salt and pepper.

Refrigerate it for 30 minutes.

Add oil to a skillet. Brown the medallions on both sides.

Add oil to a pan and sauté garlic and shallots till brown.

Add mustard, pepper, vinegar, maple syrup, tomato paste, broth, salt and pepper and bring to a boil.

It should reduce to a sauce-like consistency.

Add the beef to a plate and pour the sauce over it.

Garnish with jalapenos and cilantro and serve.

25.Avocado Mousse

Avocado mousse is a delicious and healthy dessert option. It was one of the desserts made in the episode, Devilish Desserts, which focused on desserts.

Serving size: 4

Cooking time: 30 minutes

Ingredients:

- 2 avocados, chopped
- 1 lime, zested and juiced
- 2 tablespoons lime juice
- 4 ounces cream cheese
- 2 teaspoons powdered gelatin
- 1 egg white
- 4 ounces ramekins

Instructions:

Remove pits from avocados. Then, scoop the flesh out.

Add to a processor along with lime juice and zest and whizz until smooth.

Add cream cheese and whizz.

Add to a bowl.

Beat the egg till stiff peaks form and mix with the avocado.

Add water to a bowl and sprinkle the gelatin over it.

Pour into the avocado mix and combine.

Spoon into individual serving cups and refrigerate.

Serve once the gelatin sets.

26.Roasted Apple Tart

Roasted apple tart is served to Gordon, and he surprisingly likes it. I'm sure your guests will be impressed, too, when they try this delicious tart.

Serving size: 4

Cooking time: 30 minutes

Ingredients:

- 1 stick butter
- 1 ½ cups flour
- 2 tablespoons sugar
- 3 green apples, sliced
- 1 tablespoon lemon juice
- 1 teaspoon cinnamon powder

Instructions:

Add butter, flour and 1 tablespoon sugar to a bowl and mix.

Add 3-4 tablespoons of cold water to make a firm dough.

Roll it out into a 10-inch circle.

Place it into a pie tin and flute the sides.

Slice the apples and line the pie crust.

Mix lemon juice and cinnamon and drizzle it over the apples.

Bake in a preheated 350 Fahrenheit oven for an hour.

Cool, slice and serve.

27.Tiramisu

Tiramisu is a chocolate dessert that is quite popular. It is not the easiest to make, but the effort is well worth it.

Serving size: 4

Cooking time: 30 minutes

Ingredients:

- 2 cups heavy whipping cream
- 10 ounces mascarpone cheese
- ¼ cup sugar
- 1 teaspoon vanilla extract
- 1 ½ cups espresso, cooled
- 3 tablespoons coffee liqueur
- 1 pack ladyfinger biscuits
- Cocoa powder to dust

Instructions:

Add cream to a bowl and beat till light and fluffy.

Mix mascarpone, vanilla and sugar till soft and creamy.

Mix cheese and cream till well combined.

Dip the ladyfinger biscuits in the coffee till they absorb it and line the sides of a bowl.

Add the cheese mixture in the center and smooth the top.

Dust cocoa powder over it, slice and serve.

28.Bread Pudding

Bread Pudding was served on the episode, which Gordon hated. But then, he's hard to please and generally hates everything put in front of him!

Serving size: 4

Cooking time: 30 minutes

Ingredients:

- 2 tablespoons butter
- 1 teaspoon vanilla extract
- 2 cups milk
- ¼ cup sugar
- ½ loaf brioche or sweet bread
- 2 eggs, beaten

Instructions:

Add milk, butter, sugar and vanilla to a saucepan and simmer.

Allow it to cool down.

Beat eggs and mix with the milk mixture.

Roughly tear the bread and add to a baking dish.

Pour the milk mixture all over the bread and bake in a preheated 350 Fahrenheit oven for 40 minutes.

Serve warm.

29.Goji Berry and Apple Compote

Along with the avocado mousse, this goji berry sauce is served to Gordon. The berries are rich in nutrients and go well with apples.

Serving size: 4

Cooking time: 30 minutes

Ingredients:

- 2 green apples, peeled and chopped
- ½ cup goji berries
- 2 tablespoons cinnamon powder
- ½ cup water

Instructions:

Add water, cinnamon, apples and berries to a pot and boil.

Simmer and cook till soft.

Mash half the mixture and allow it to cool down.

Serve with sweet Greek yogurt.

30.Raspberry Salad

Raspberries are also featured in the episode. They are healthy and delicious and perfect to make salads.

Serving size: 4-6

Cooking time: 5 minutes

Ingredients:

- 10 ounces raspberries
- 4 ounces blackberries
- 4 ounces strawberries
- 2 cups cherries
- 1 lime, juiced and zested
- 1 tablespoon honey
- Mint leaves

Instructions:

Halve the berries and add to a bowl.

Mix lime juice, zest and honey and drizzle over the berries and toss.

Serve with a sprinkling of mint leaves.

Conclusion

Thank you for choosing this book, and I hope you enjoyed reading it.

Hell's Kitchen introduced us to a lot of great recipes, and I tried to include the best ones.

I really hope you will have a good time trying them out. Feel free to switch up the ingredients and come up with recipes of your own!

Bon Appetit!

Made in the USA
Las Vegas, NV
08 February 2024

85478697R00044